When God Showed Up

When God Showed Up

DEBBIE WOOD

XULON ELITE

Xulon Press
2301 Lucien Way #415
Maitland, FL 32751
407.339.4217

www.xulonpress.com

© 2021 by Debbie Wood

All rights reserved solely by the author. The author guarantees all contents are original and do not infringe upon the legal rights of any other person or work. No part of this book may be reproduced in any form without the permission of the author. The views expressed in this book are not necessarily those of the publisher.

Due to the changing nature of the Internet, if there are any web addresses, links, or URLs included in this manuscript, these may have been altered and may no longer be accessible. The views and opinions shared in this book belong solely to the author and do not necessarily reflect those of the publisher. The publisher therefore disclaims responsibility for the views or opinions expressed within the work.

Scripture quotations taken from the Holy Bible, New International Version (NIV). Copyright © 1973, 1978, 1984, 2011 by Biblica, Inc.™. Used by permission. All rights reserved.

Printed in the United States of America

Paperback ISBN-13: 978-1-6628-4087-6
Hard Cover ISBN-13: 978-1-6628-4088-3
Ebook ISBN-13: 978-1-6628-4089-0

Cover art by Sara Wood

When God Showed Up is dedicated to:

The Lord God Almighty
My husband, Damon
Abi Gordon

Contents

Preface ix
Introduction... xi
Chapter 1 - Foundation of Faith 1
Chapter 2 - A Sacrifice of Thanksgiving............... 5
Chapter 3 – Worry, Willpower or Worship 9
Chapter 4 – Attitude 13
Chapter 5 - Strong and Loving 17
Chapter 6 - Purpose in Pain 19
Chapter 7 - The Body of Christ 23
Chapter 8 – Marriage 27
Chapter 9 - Teachable Moments 31
Chapter 10 - Visual Aids............................. 39
Chapter 11 – Victory................................. 43
Epilogue 47

Preface

When God Showed Up is birthed from feedback I received as I walked through a season that included a battle with idiopathic neuropathy and stage four cancer, both of which were dramatic surprises. The story I want to tell here isn't the medical one, but the spiritual one. It is said that being faced with an unexpected battle reveals one's true nature and what I truly believe about God. Do I react in fear or respond in faith? *When God Showed Up* is simply my true story of faith, reflected in supernatural peace and joy.

I pray the lessons and stories in *When God Showed Up* will be an encouragement to you. Some might even challenge you. If you are not facing a battle now, are you confident of how you will face one? I did not see either of mine coming; you might not either. Maybe something you read here will help you be more battle ready. If you are in a battle now, who is winning? When others see your battle do they see faith? When facing a battle with faith God always wins! And, maybe something you read here will open your eyes more to the reality that God wants to show up in your life too, in times of peace and in battle. He can and will use anything you experience to help you know him better, to change you into the likeness of Jesus, to use your story as a testimony to others.

Introduction

⸺⧖⸺

When God Showed Up is not about a crisis of faith or about spiritual warfare. Battle is simply my word for a trial, difficulty, challenge, or test of faith. I love the idea of winning! God's Word makes it clear that battles will come and that He allows battles for His purposes. For example, in 1 Peter 1:6-7, I learn that battles refine my faith and prove it genuine and result in praise, glory, and honor when Jesus Christ is revealed. In James 1:2-4, I learn I can even consider battles as pure joy because I know that the testing of my faith develops perseverance, which leads to my becoming mature and complete in my spiritual transformation, not lacking anything. Romans 8:35-38 reminds me I am never separated from the love of Christ, not even in battle. In fact, I am more than a conqueror! I get to enjoy a victory because God always wins. It is not true that God gives does not give me more than we can handle. He allows more than I can handle so I can learn to trust him, to know him better, so I can be transformed.

I believe my story played out the way it did because I was ready for the battle, even though I didn't see it coming. God knew before I was born that I would face this battle. He knew what I would need to learn, how I would need to grow spiritually, and how well I would need to know him to be able to manage the battle with a mindset of victory based on faith.

When God Showed Up is, first, about the value and process of spiritual growth through a relationship with Jesus Christ grounded in the Word <u>before</u> a battle—being battle ready. I share some key lessons I learned over the years not necessarily knowing why I would need these lessons. God knew. God calls me, even commands me to build up my faith. As I obey, He rewards faith with victory in battle. I trust him; he comes through, always. God always wins. I believe it is because I was battle ready that, when the battle hit and all throughout it, my heart, mind and spirit were ready for Him to show up, to even be expectant. If I am too busy or distracted by worry or fear I won't be able to see when God shows up. If I am focused on the negatives I won't be able to see the positives. Faith frees me to see God show up.

When God Showed Up is also a collection of experiences of God showing up during this battle. Sure, He has shown up many times in my life, in many different settings. But it was during this battle that his showing up was the most dramatic and impactful. He showed up during specific medical tests, using them as teachable moments, sometimes even as visual aids. I learned new things about him and who I am or can be in him, about how he wants to engage with me, about how he wants to use me to help others, to further his kingdom. God can use anything, any experience he wants as a means to show up; and that he did.

Chapter 1

Foundation of Faith

Being battle ready means my faith is strong enough for battle. I know from the outset who wins, which means I have an accurate lens of who God is. What I believe to be true about God, or my spiritual lens, is accurately based on His Word. Knowing and believing the promises of His Word means I can trust He will be with me, for me, and that He has a divine purpose for everything he allows. It means I can know that He will always be bigger than any battle. When this is true, as I face a battle, my faith is strengthened during it-not weakened. God seems near, not far or absent. I love God more, not less. God is honored more, not less. Others see joy in my story, not complaining or throwing a pity party. My story is about God, not me. They see that Jesus is real, that faith matters!

A biblical lesson on battle readiness is found in Luke 6:47-48. This passage says, "As for everyone who comes to me and hears my words and puts them into practice, I will show you what they are like. They are like a man building a house, who dug down deep and laid the foundation on rock. When a flood came, the torrent struck that house but could not shake it, because it was well built" (NIV).

When I visualize this passage in Luke, I see it from a distance. I see the storm and the house. The storm is any challenging journey. The house is my life story as it is lived out and as others see it. Then, as if the land is sliced open, I can see the foundation the house is built upon and that the foundation does in fact dig deep into the rock. It isn't enough to just build a foundation; I have to dig deep enough to get to the rock for a foundation that lasts and holds through storms (or rather, a battle).

My application of this verse is that as I choose to read, study, meditate, and memorize His Word and am obedient to walk in God's truth—intentionally, deeply, and consistently— the stronger and deeper my faith becomes. My spiritual diet gives me spiritual strength and energy to grow in righteousness. His Word is living and active. When I spend time in the Word, I am not just reading; I am intentionally spending time with the One who is the Word.

It is also true God's Word encourages—even commands— me to build godliness. 1 Timothy 4:7 tells me to train myself to be godly. 2 Timothy 3:16-17 tells me of the power of knowing and living out the truth of His Word, that it is useful for actual life change, including training in righteousness, so that I will be thoroughly equipped. Jude 1:20 tells me to build myself up in my most holy faith. I have a role to play in being battle-ready. Physical fitness and spiritual fitness are both choices I need to make, and both contribute to quality of life now and for the future.

God will show up whether I am walking in faith or not because He is the One who decides. For me, there was a time many years ago when I had walked away from God, losing the battle of faith. After seven years, without my asking for it, God showed up and simply called me to trust Him. Somehow, He knew I was ready then.

What an honor it is, though, to be so strong spiritually that when a battle hits, I can anticipate God doing something amazing. This is being battle ready.

Sometimes it is hard to see the foundation building when it is happening; sometimes I only see that it happened when I look back at who I used to be or how I used to act. I see that I am different, transformed, and actually more like Jesus!

CHAPTER 2

A Sacrifice of Thanksgiving

―――∝―――

*B*eing battle ready means I can be thankful for any battle. I know every battle I face is allowed by a sovereign God for His divine purposes. When I truly believe that God is always good, even in a battle, and that He will redeem any battle for His purposes, I can choose to be thankful for it, even when I don't or can't know how hard the battle will be or how long the battle will last. When facing a battle, being thankful reveals faith that God's got this and is about to do something new.

Sometimes thankfulness requires faith. As a human, when I face a battle, it would seem normal to have a negative reaction. Battle are bad, right? God is good all the time, which means when He allows a battle, He has something good in mind for me, which means I can be thankful. Psalm 50:23 tells this story. This verse says, "He who sacrifices thank offerings honors me, and he prepares the way so that I may show him the salvation of God" (NIV). Let's break it down.

A sacrifice means I am giving up or surrendering something that is mine—something I want or even need. This is why it is considered a sacrifice. If I did not want or need whatever I was offering, it wouldn't really matter; it wouldn't be sacrificial.

An offering is the actual act of giving something to God, something specific. A sacrifice of a "thank offering" (also known as a thanksgiving offering) means I am intentionally <u>choosing</u> thankfulness because I would not normally be thankful for it so it would not come naturally. I would not normally, as a human, be thankful for a battle. I'd rather have an easy life, right? Being thankful for a battle is a spiritual choice based on the right lens of who God is.

As a human with a sin nature, it can be easy for me to want to "own" or navigate my life's battles, making them all about me and how I want them to turn out. Also, when faced with a battle, it can be easy to have a negative reaction. I am human, after all. Human emotion is natural and even God-given. It is how I manage my emotions that matters, certainly as they impact my attitude. More on this later. I can become self-centered, angry, bitter, fearful, worried, or cynical. I can throw a pity party complete with less-than healthy food and beverages or in how I spend my time. The world offers plenty of distractions, and I have an enemy that will convince me to make a godless choice.

I can also question God in the midst of a battle. Does He know? Does He care? Why would He allow this? Where is He? Doesn't He know how I feel, how hard this is? Can He help? Will He help? Lots of questions. It is the fact that I am a Christ-follower that I have the supernatural option to address battles differently by not relying on humanity.

When I choose to thank God for a given battle, this reflects faith, and faith always honors God. Faith releases me to see God work, to trust that He will work, that He will win. Everything

He does in my life or allows me to experience is part of my salvation story, my testimony of ongoing sanctification and becoming like Christ. God never wastes anything I give Him in faith, especially an offering. He can and will use anything and everything I face—any battle—to accomplish His purposes in me and through me, bringing glory to His name. This is the power of thanksgiving.

Chapter 3

Worry, Willpower, or Worship

───────∝───────

*B*eing battle ready means I can worship God in the midst of it. When faced with a battle of any kind, either I can own it or let God own it. By "owning it," I mean who is controlling it. If I own it, the result usually means focusing on myself by <u>worrying</u> about it or trying to win it on my own through <u>willpower</u>. With worry, no one does anything because worry is passively destructive. With willpower, it is up to me to gut it out or try to change my circumstances somehow on my own. Relying on willpower is exhausting and, in some cases, surely leads to losing a battle; it is actively destructive.

If I let God "own" my battle, now it is a whole new thing! When I understand God's character and that He can redeem anything for His purposes, I can then give my battle to God in <u>worship</u>. It may be worship by faith as I journey through a battle; this worship is by choice. Attitude and faith are both choices. I continue to learn this truth by studying some biblical heroes who also experienced a battle and who also chose worship:

- There is the story of King Jehoshaphat in 2 Chronicles 20. In verse 15, God reminds him that the battle is his.

- Next is Job. Over an apparently short period of time, he loses all his flocks, attending servants, and then all his children (Job 1:13-19). Job's response was at first naturally human; he tore his robes and shaved his head (a symbol of grief). But then he fell to the ground in worship and said: "Naked I came from my mother's womb, and naked I will depart. The Lord gave and the Lord has taken away; may the name of the LORD be praised" (Job 1:21, NIV).
- In the Book of Daniel, Shadrach, Meshach and Abednego replied to the king, "O Nebuchadnezzar, we do not need to defend ourselves before you in this matter. If we are thrown into the blazing furnace, the God we serve is able to save us from it, and he will rescue us from your hand O king. But even if he does not, we want you to know, O king that we will not serve your gods or worship the image of gold you have set up" (Dan. 316-18, NIV). These young men knew who to worship, that God alone is worthy! This right lens lead to the battle victory in the flames. Isn't it fascinating that the only thing that burned in the furnace—or was impacted at all—was the ropes that bound them?!
- The prophet Habakkuk, seeing his land and people ravaged by the Chaldeans in Habakkuk 3:17-18, said: "Though the fig tree does not bud and there are no grapes on the vines, though the olive crop fails and the fields produce no food, though there are no sheep in the pen and no cattle in the stall, yet I will rejoice in the Lord, I will be joyful in God my Savior" (NIV).
- And finally, there is Stephen. In Acts 7:55-60, we read, "But being full of the Holy Spirit, he gazed intently

into heaven and saw the glory of God, and Jesus standing at the right hand of God; and he said, 'Behold, I see the heavens opened up and the Son of Man standing at the right hand of God.' But they cried out with a loud voice, and covered their ears and rushed at him with one impulse. When they had driven him out of the city, they began stoning him; and the witnesses laid aside their robes at the feet of a young man named Saul. They went on stoning Stephen as he called on the Lord and said, 'Lord Jesus, receive my spirit!' Then falling on his knees, he cried out with a loud voice, 'Lord, do not hold this sin against them!' Having said this, he fell asleep" (NIV).

What is true about all these stories? Each of these men chose to trust God instead of themselves. They chose worship instead of worry or willpower. The key for me is to make the same righteous choice. I want to know God so well that as soon as a battle hits, I turn to worship before worry or willpower ever sets in ... because one of them will, eventually, if I'm not careful, if I'm not intentional. If I don't <u>choose</u> worship, I have an enemy that will convince me that worry or willpower are my only choices.

I choose to put a "stake in the ground" and decide that although I will never fully understand who God is or how He acts or what He allows, that that is okay. I know enough- enough to trust. I will not trust someone I don't believe is worthy of it. The same is true of worship; I have to decide He is worthy, always. I am commanded to worship, never with conditions.

I am learning the value of the spiritual discipline of worship; it needs to be a familiar place and practice. I believe worship is the one spiritual discipline that most increases my view or my lens of God. Praise is about what God <u>does</u>; worship is about who God is. I believe it is valuable for me to know God beyond what He does or can do for me. I always need to keep learning more of who God is in His awesome, unchanging nature-the God who is the same during times of peace and during a battle. The only reason I ever struggle with anything—a battle or simply sin—is because I still don't know God well enough. Knowing God, spending time in His presence, changes me. So, the more I invest in expanding my view of all that God is as a daily practice of worship, the more accurate my lens when a battle hits. I need to view my battle through the lens of who God is, not determine my view of God through the lens of the battle.

I have also learned that there is no such thing as true worship and ... anything else. There is no multitasking in worship. We humans can only concentrate on one thing at a time. Sure, I love to listen to worship music while I do chores or a puzzle, but then my focus is not purely on worship. Listening to "worship" music is not necessarily spending time in worship. Where is that other blue piece in this puzzle? What did I come into the room to get? Oh, look at the cute baby on social media! God is honored and revealed in my true worship when it is just and only about Him. I believe it is in these moments of pure worship that I experience the most spiritual transformation because it is in pure worship I get the clearest picture of how big and magnificent God is. The bigger my picture of God, the smaller my picture of anyone or anything else including of me. The biggest problem of faith—especially when facing a battle—is an inadequate view of God. The habit of true worship is the answer.

Chapter 4

Attitude

---—∝---—

*B*eing battle ready means I understand the power of attitude. Without getting too technical or too deep into psychology, I am learning two things about attitude. First, attitude is different from feeling, and second, attitude is a choice. For example, happiness is a feeling, while joy is an attitude. I <u>choose</u> attitude, and then, based on that attitude, I (hopefully) <u>control</u> how I feel, including feeling happy. I think happiness is circumstantial or conditional and momentary, while joy is—or can be—unconditional and can be chosen anytime from a place of faith, even during a battle. And in God's kingdom, joy is also supernatural, not dependent on any circumstance. He wouldn't command me to be joyful always (1 Thes. 5:16) if it wasn't possible. God would never command something He won't equip me to do. He will command me to make choices that require <u>His</u> supernatural presence. I need to keep remembering that I have the indwelling Holy Spirit who empowers me and my choices.

Back when I was a corporate trainer, my favorite topic to present was the four quotients, also referred to as the four capacities, the four types of intelligence, or the four steps to wellness. The idea is, as a human, there are four possible ways I can change who I am and how I live. Every day all four are at play. Every aspect of my human life change falls into at least one of these quotients. This is such a powerful and empowering topic, especially when I bring God into it! (Maybe I will write a book about it!) Keep in mind, this is my interpretation of this content.

The four quotients are: emotional (EQ), spiritual (SQ), mental (IQ), and physical (PQ). My EQ is my capacity to control my emotions and understand others' emotions. My SQ is my capacity for faith and all things spiritual or all things bigger than or beyond me. My IQ is my capacity for learning and reasoning. My PQ is my capacity for physical wellness related to diet, rest, and exercise.

Not only will each quotient impact my daily choices, any of the four can work in conjunction with each other, even all four at once. For example, let's say I start having a weird pain in my chest (PQ). I decide to do my own research to learn what it could be (IQ). Yes, I google it. I read that what I am experiencing could be a symptom of a heart attack, which causes me to be fearful (EQ). I start to question why a loving God would allow this horrible physical ailment (SQ). There is actually nothing really wrong with me, except maybe something I ate; but in a matter of minutes, I have tapped into all four quotients.

All four quotients can be found throughout scripture and are part of how God engages with us and wants us to engage with Him. All four are God-given, based on my interpretation of the greatest commandment mentioned in Mark 12 which addresses the heart, soul, mind, and strength. I am commanded to love God with all of me-with all four quotients. This means He will help me in understanding and building them. Remember, another word for quotients is "capacity." God will help me increase my capacity for each quotient as each can be developed independently and in conjunction with each other. Not only can all four can be found throughout His Word, I can experience all four even as I read and respond to a particular passage. For example, when I study God's Word, I am using IQ because I use my mind to read and understand the truth intellectually, my spirit relates to the truth spiritually (SQ), even my heart might react emotionally (EQ). I can respond to truth physically (PQ) by kneeling in prayer, opening my hands in surrender, or raising my arms in worship. God cares about my emotions, my faith, my intellect, and my body—and how I treat them or improve them. I also have the freewill option to ignore them.

One of the many powerful aspects of understanding the four quotients is that all four can have an impact on attitude—and my capacity to choose the right attitude, especially in a battle. Attitude can be driven by emotions (EQ), faith (SQ), thoughts (IQ), and simply how I feel physically (PQ).

In any battle, it is my chosen attitude that impacts how I manage that battle and how it impacts me, good or bad. Every battle will change me one way or another. It is my attitude about the battle itself and also my attitude about God—who He is in the midst of a battle, and what He might want to accomplish through a battle. Again, God never wastes anything—including a battle—if it is offered to Him in faith. He will always have a divine purpose if I allow it by faith.

The stronger I am in all four quotients, the more I walk a life of victory, reflecting in daily life the truth that a relationship with Jesus Christ does, in fact, make a difference in this life. Not only do I benefit by making it through a battle with joy instead of worry or fear, but others benefit as they see this joy and realize that it is possible with God. Remember, God says that a life of joy is possible! His Word contains approximately 200 verses about joy, depending on your translation. The power to choose joy became a huge part of my battle. It was nothing less than supernatural through the Holy Spirit. God's Word said it, and I believed it, so I chose it. And, during the especially hard times, it was His Spirit in me, empowering my joy. Attitude is a choice. Faith is a choice. Joy is a choice.

Chapter 5

Strong and Loving

―――――∝―――――

One of foundation-laying truths I am still learning came during a particularly difficult day. I was at a place where, physically, it was more than I could handle. Battles can have ups and down; this was a down. Who is God in moments like this?

Then God showed up. He reminded me of a verse He had me study a while back. Psalm 62:11-12 says, "One thing God has spoken, two things I have heard: that you O God, are strong, and that you O Lord, are loving. Surely, you will reward each person according to what he has done" (NIV). He brought to mind that, as a Christ-follower, whenever I doubt Him or struggle in my faith in Him, it is only for one reason: I don't know Him well enough in two key components of His character-either I believe He <u>can't</u> help me or He <u>won't</u>. He either doesn't have the <u>power,</u> or He doesn't <u>care</u>. If I believe He can't help, it means He is not all-powerful or sovereign, or that He simply doesn't know what to do to help. It causes me to question that one of His names means "the God who heals." If I believe He won't help me, it means His love is conditional, or

He has better things to do, or other people matter more—perhaps, those more godly? Maybe I'm not worthy enough.

Fortunately, during this season, I did believe God is strong enough and loving enough; in fact, more than enough. He brought a song to mind called "Enough" by Chris Tomlin. The chorus of this song says, *"All of You is more than enough for all of me, For every thirst and every need, You satisfy me with Your love, And all I have in You is more than enough."* It is God's power <u>and</u> love that helped me, ministered to me, and strengthened me. It was both that brought me through the rough parts for His glory sake.

Another layer is having to trust in God's character (His power and love) in how and when He chooses to display it. He may manifest power and love in ways I don't anticipate or in the timing I expect or hope for. It is exactly when I face the hardest aspects of a battle, like excruciating pain that God does not take away, that trusting in God's character matters most.

It is true that what I think about God is the most important aspect of my entire life, which is certainly true since it determines eternity, not to mention the quality of daily life. For years I made the mistake of allowing a battle to be my lens for how I defined God instead of having an accurate knowledge of God to be my lens in defining my battle. Having a lens of God's ability and desire to help me in battle matters. Trust His character and not how I feel about His character.

Chapter 6

Purpose in Pain

---∝---

*B*eing battle ready means I can trust God with new thresholds. In my case, this was my threshold for physical pain. Most of the pain I continue to experience is excruciating pain in my right foot due to a neuropathy issue we are still trying to figure out. Sometimes the pain was from the side effects of a lot of chemo. Sometimes it was from so many needles. I hate needles. A few times, the pain was due to a medical procedure. What I learned about managing pain, letting Jesus use my pain, is easily the most life-changing victory of my battle, especially as it is ongoing-three and half years going.

Early on, on a particular Sunday morning, one of our teaching pastors just happened to speak about suffering well. Note, there are no coincidences in God. After the sermon, he was available to pray. I told him about my foot pain, how bad it is when it flares up, and asked him why God might be allowing this pain that is sometimes so excruciating. He thought for a moment, then said something to the effect of, perhaps, I was being allowed an opportunity to participate in the sufferings of Christ. This hit me hard! I never thought of this before now. I didn't know how to process it in the moment. I had certainly read that scripture many times that he mentioned in his sermon but never really understood it-not yet. I went home and looked up the scriptures that he referenced.

> *"I want to know Christ and the power of his resurrection and the fellowship of sharing in his sufferings, becoming like him in his death, and so, somehow, to attain to the resurrection from the dead" (Philippians 3:10-11, NIV).*

> *"Dear friends, do not be surprised at the painful battle you are suffering, as though something strange were happening to you. But rejoice that you participate in the sufferings of Christ, so that you may be overjoyed when his glory is revealed" (1 Peter 4:12-13, NIV).*

As I read these scriptures, I knew God was teaching me something, revealing some new truth, but at this point, I couldn't quite figure it out. It was in the midst of an especially challenging pain episode that God showed up and made these scriptures come alive. In a moment of excruciating pain during a medical procedure, I heard Jesus say, in effect, He was allowing me to feel this much pain because it was a gift of a very small taste of what He was willing to endure when He was tortured and crucified for me. Talk about practical application! I understood more than ever before how much He loved me as He suffered for me, that He would willingly feel that much pain for me. I knew it because I felt it, at least a little. I felt loved because God showed up.

It was in yet another episode of pain that I was meditating on these same scriptures. God showed up with a new revelation. Never before had I considered when Jesus was being whipped so brutally and then crucified, what or who was He looking at? In this moment, as I considered His pain and mine, He was looking at me. He took every whip and every nail for me. What He felt physically, He felt for me.

Yet another time, God showed up in an episode of pain but with a different message. This time, I was out for a long walk alone and enjoying a time of prayer. Then the pain started again in my right foot. I was two miles from home and had to hobble the rest of the way since I was on a trail. In that much pain, and being human, I started to cry. The pain was great, and I was tired of great pain. I really, really wanted the pain to stop. I begged God to make it stop. Then God showed up. It was as if I could hear Him say something to the effect of He wanted me to want Him more than I want the pain to stop. It was a lesson of perspective in intensity. How much do I truly desire Jesus? It is hard to define a feeling or a desire or a need until there is application. As much as I needed to feel less pain, I needed Jesus more.

Another time, I was out for a walk and the neuropathy pain hit again. I was learning to expect God to show up during these moments. This time, God said He wanted me to use the awareness of pain to pray in empathy for others, especially those I knew who were also dealing with physical pain in some way. Two specific people came to mind. Being in intense pain can make a person self-focused. Interceding for others distracted me from how much pain I was in and instead empowered empathetic prayer.

God shows up in times of physical pain to help me understand His love, to choose to desire Him on a deeper level, and to drive me to empathetic intercession for others.

Chapter 7

The Body of Christ

───────⚭───────

*B*eing battle ready means I am not fighting alone. There are no lone soldiers in God's kingdom. Another set of lessons that I am still learning to grasp is understanding the value and power of the body of Christ. There are about one hundred verses in the Bible using the phrase "one another," with almost half being specific commands on how to relate to one another. It matters to God not only <u>that</u> I engage with other Christ-followers, but also <u>how</u> I engage with them. Simply showing up at church is not what God meant. We are supposed to love each other like Jesus, need each other, and help each other, to be honest and vulnerable and available. Unity in community is how God designed His kingdom and His Body to work, to be strengthened, and to grow in impact to a watching and needy world full of isolation.

Being a part of the body of Christ incudes gathering corporately, like on Sunday mornings, and in smaller interactions, like a bible study, home group, dinner fellowship, or simply having coffee or breaking bread. Corporate and personal interactions are both important for their own reasons.

There had been times during my long spiritual journey when I did not rely on other Christ-followers through battles because of my pride. I didn't want to admit a weakness—certainly not a sin—or appear too needy or bother them. Maybe I didn't want them to feel bad for me. I didn't want to make them feel miserable. I'm doing them a favor by not sharing. In some cases, I even thought it was none of their business, or that suffering was a private matter, especially if my sin was involved. Or, they didn't seem to have any needs of their own, so it would feel lopsided if I was the only needy one in the relationship or group. Some people seemed too busy or preoccupied with their own lives. I didn't ask them, of course; I just assumed. And, because I did not know God well, my battles were always only about me, me complaining, again. That gets old for anyone.

The impact of keeping my battles to myself back then really only God knows. I remember, though, times of deep loneliness, depression, worry, and even thoughts of suicide that might have been mitigated or even prevented if I would have simply invited others into the battle.

I was learning I couldn't walk rightly with God without other Christ-followers. The idea of the body of Christ matters to Christ Himself, clearly spelled out in passages like Romans 12. And needing others has to go both ways. I need them; they need me—this is the body of Christ at its best, truly loving one another and building each other up. As a Christ-follower, being forgiven, redeemed, and loved gives me the freedom to be humble, honest, and transparent. Christ's love should compel me to love others, letting them be humble, honest, and transparent with me. We build one another up.

As I was humbly open to this idea during the cancer battle, God brought so many amazing Christ-followers all along the way, each with their own way to bless, help, or minister. I admit, it was humbling to be so needy and unable to reciprocate at the time, but it was beautiful to watch them be blessed by being a blessing! Helping me was their walking in obedience to loving others and a pathway to walk out their spiritual gifting and the fruit of the Spirit. If I don't let others in, we both lose.

God shows up through His body. Early in my cancer battle, two of our pastors arranged for me to be prayed over by the other pastors, elders, and others after the services were over. I sat in a chair while I was anointed with oil and a few laid hands. Several others gathered, about twenty in total, nearby. It was a James 5:14 moment.

Then God showed up in the form of a vision. As people prayed for me, I had a vision of several enemy spirits showing up in the room, up by the ceiling, all considering an attack. But then they saw something that spooked them; they were all looking at the same thing. As I followed their gaze, I envisioned a very large, heavenly being standing beside me with his sword out. As they saw the army praying for me and this heavenly being, they knew they didn't stand a chance and left.

Being prayed over like this was an amazing time of praise, worship, thanksgiving, and, of course, prayers for healing and claiming God's promises. From this God sighting, I was reminded that my health battles are not just physical in nature; they are, or can be, also a spiritual battle. The great enemy of Christ is okay with my having a physical battle because he knows many Christ-followers have lost their way in the midst of one. It was after this moment of prayer that I never felt another spiritual attack during this battle.

I am convinced that one of the reasons my battle played out the way it did as a positive experience spiritually was because others were praying for me. There was simply a supernatural force at work. The prayers of the righteous are powerful and effective according to James 5:16. I know this firsthand. There were so many times I simply felt strengthened in my spirit, and I could not explain why except for the prayers of the saints. God shows up through people, if I let them. I don't ever want to be so prideful that I don't let others grow spiritually by letting them be the body of Christ for me.

Chapter 8

Marriage

The most important human relationship I have is with my spouse, Damon. This is true for all of us who are married. Marriage is God's one covenant relationship. Marriage is the metaphor He uses to convey the spiritual relationship of Christ and His Church. I mention marriage here because it is a big part of my victory-of our victory. Damon and I fought this battle arm in arm. Just as having a strong faith helps me manage battles well, the same is true of marriage. Battles can test faith and a marriage.

A huge piece of strength in marriage is the strength of faith, with each of us being intentional and proactive in our individual spiritual journeys with the Lord. We learned—better late than never—that pretty much all of our marriage issues are tied to our individual spiritual journeys. The further away from God, the more we struggled; the closer in our individual relationships with God, the more our marriage was strengthened. Simple concept.

I love the idea that the "marriage" of Christ and His church is what my marriage should look like (Eph. 5:22-27). I submit to my husband as to the Lord, as the church submits to Christ;

my husband loves me just as Christ loved the church and gave Himself up for her. I love the idea of the gospel in the context of marriage, that oneness in marriage is like the oneness of Christ and His church as found in verses thirty-one and thirty-two. The connection of the gospel and marriage gives our marriage a deeper meaning, a higher value, a testimony. The guidelines of submission and love are powerfully true for the Christ-follower and a marriage. I may not like the idea of submission, but I can trust it.

Another lesson I am learning is that relationships, especially marriage, are fluid. Relationships that matter are never stagnant. A relationship is either getting stronger or weaker over time, closer or farther apart. Deeper or more shallow. In a Christian marriage, there is the word "oneness." Genesis 2:24 uses the phrase "become one flesh." Matthew 19:6 says we are longer two, but one. Isolation is easy; oneness takes work. Isolation can happen passively; oneness takes intentionality. When Damon and I are intentional about moving toward oneness, there are blessings! Certainly we each benefit in many ways, and we benefit together in many ways. It has been such a joy to see how our marriage has changed over the years, where we are now, and therefore, the desire to see it grow even more.

I love being married. Thirty-nine years into it as of this writing, Damon and I have intentionally worked (most of the time) to get where we are. Just like faith, a strong, godly marriage is not by accident. As we have chosen to honor God in our commitment to our marriage, we are motivated to strengthen it-for it to be the covenant relationship God intended for His kingdom purposes, for us, and for those watching.

Often when we are out in public, say at a restaurant, folks walk up to us and tell us that we clearly have an "adorable" relationship, or that we are clearly happily married, or obviously in love. We even had a body language expert approach us once to say that he had been watching us from across the room and felt compelled to give us feedback that we are clearly in love. Then some ask how long we have been married. When we tell them how long, their mouths drop open. Some say they don't know of anyone who has lasted that long. I love it when they ask why or how! For us, it is an easy answer. Even if they don't ask, we still give an answer-Jesus Christ!

Marriage in God's way is a great pathway to the gospel. Damon and I both believe our keys to a great marriage are God and giggles. Clearly, marriage should be God-centered, and marriage should be fun. We giggle a lot. You should see us; it's adorable! Each marriage has its own unique version or display of oneness. For us, we are just silly. We even have our own handshake.

An important layer to consider in the idea of a godly marriage being a testimony to others, especially during a battle, is its testimony to our adult children. Do we have the marriage we want them to have? They *are* watching and learning, the good and the bad.

Because Damon and I have been intentional about investing in our marriage, it was, and is, strong enough to handle the battle, even as the neuropathy one continues. The biggest test was getting the very serious final cancer diagnosis as there was no guarantee I would survive. When he and I first had to process the diagnosis together, we both burst into tears, initially in shock of the scary news, and simply held each other. We are human. Then, without planning it or even choosing it, we found ourselves praying, giving thanks, and worshipping. We each came out of this moment completely convinced of God's sovereignty. We knew He had this journey and would use it for His purposes. We knew this battle was God's, not just ours, and that He would have the victory. This moment birthed the phrase we often speak since: "God knows!" It has become our mantra for any battle. He always knows exactly what I face in battle, and He knows the outcome, always. God always wins.

God showed up for Damon by giving him peace, faith, strength, a clear mind to keep all the facts and my meds straight, and helping him keep his great playfulness. God used Damon as he would speak biblical truth to me, prayed with me at least daily, and always held me through the really, really hard parts.

A godly marriage is fulfilling to each of us and is an awesome pathway to a gospel conversation, reflecting the truth of God's Word and His presence in hope and help. Through our individual spiritual growth, commitment to the body of Christ in a local church, intentional date nights, and investing in learning about marriage through amazing events like the Weekend to Remember marriage getaway, Damon and I are increasingly enjoying a victorious Christian marriage. Godly marriage rocks!

Chapter 9

Teachable Moments

There were many times throughout my battle with both medical issues that God showed up in unique and intimate teachable moments. These moments were times of God revealing something about Himself and or something about me. Here are those stories.

Good enough? Halfway through chemo I was in full remission. My first thought was "Praise the Lord!" Then it was, "The battle is over!" I asked my oncologist if this meant I was done with chemo, if I could skip the second half. Isn't full remission good enough? Nope. Then I asked if it meant we could use an easier chemo option. Nope. He said I had to finish the full inpatient treatment to ensure not only full remission, but to actually be cured. I needed to realize that remission, even full remission, isn't good enough.

As I walked down the long hallway to the cancer ward again, thinking about how challenging the next chemo rounds would be, I found myself complaining. Why couldn't remission be good enough? Then God showed up. He reminded me I should never settle for good enough, not in my health, and never with Him. A "good enough" faith. A "good enough" quiet time. A "good enough" prayer time. The idea of settling for "good enough" can penetrate any aspect of my life: my diet, exercise, rest, marriage, work ethic, and so on. There is no "good enough" in God.

God knew that. For the better part of a year before cancer, I had been asking for the heart of the early disciples. For example, Acts 4:13 says, "When they saw the courage of Peter and John and realized that they were unschooled, ordinary men, they were astonished and they took note that these men had been with Jesus" (NIV). And then verse twenty says, "For we cannot help speaking about what we have seen and heard" (NIV). Yes, Jesus' early disciples died for Him, but first they lived for Him. They knew Jesus, and it changed them. They knew Jesus, and other people knew that they knew Jesus. I wanted this-to know Jesus in this life-changing way.

Yes, I am a work in progress. Jesus has died for my sin, yet I still sin. I won't be "cured" from my sin nature until Heaven. In the meantime, I can't settle for good enough, not in any way that matters. Jesus' death and resurrection mean more than that. I don't ever want to settle for a "good enough" testimony or faith. I want my life to matter more than that, to truly impact other's lives for Christ by choosing to finish and win my battles.

Defenseless. One day, sitting in my hospital bed, looking at the white board where my team (medical staff and Damon) kept a record of my daily three blood counts, I noticed that they were all zeros. My body was no longer producing white cells, hemoglobin, or platelets. I processed what this implied: being defenseless. If I was exposed to any germ or bacteria, I would have no defense, and an infection could become septic, which could be life-threatening.

As I considered the word "defenseless" and how helpless I felt, God showed up. He reminded me that, in Him, there are no zeroes. I am never actually defenseless in any sense of the word because He is in charge. <u>Nothing</u> can attack me without His consent and purpose—nothing physical or spiritual. Every single physical and spiritual issue I face He already knows about and is working in the midst of it, if I allow Him to. He is always with me and for me. And in Him, I always have the victory. He is my champion in every way forever. God always wins!

Anemia. During the cancer battle, my oncologist highly encouraged me to exercise every day I was home, including cardio and weights. But I had to redefine what "exercise" meant. It wasn't until late in the battle that I even wanted to go to the gym or felt I had the energy. During my first time back at the gym, I struggled to lift a hand weight that used to be super easy. I admit I was a bit discouraged. Surely I am stronger than this! I tried a lighter weight-same result. Bigger sigh. I realized it wasn't that the weight was too heavy, but that I was unable to breathe while trying. I thought I would try light cardio instead. Not too far into it, the breathlessness started, a familiar feeling. My new "normal" of exercise was limited by what I now knew was a low level of hemoglobin in my blood, how this whole battle started. All my blood counts were struggling to recover. For context, low hemoglobin means less oxygen. When hemoglobin drops low enough, this condition is called anemia. Apparently, the cancer and the chemo both contributed to my anemia. One sign of anemia is breathlessness on exertion.

As I pondered the impact of anemia on my fitness goals, God showed up. He spoke to me about the idea that I could experience spiritual anemia. God taught me that, just as my <u>body</u> needs blood flowing, my <u>soul</u> needs the Spirit flowing. I didn't have control over my hemoglobin, but I do have control over how much I let the Spirit have His way in my life, flowing to me and through me.

They say cancer is a silent killer because, too many times, you don't know you have it until it is too late. I came close. No symptoms until stage four. I think sin can work the same way. I can get so busy with life, even Christian service, and do it just fine all on my own. My own strength, gifts, abilities, and money. I might slowly spend less and less time with the Lord and slowly drift further and further away from holiness. A little distance from God can slowly become wider and longer over time. It can happen so slowly I probably don't even notice. I may not notice until something happens, a symptom shows up. It can be a small symptom or a big one. I can find myself unexpectedly tempted by something, perhaps even something I thought I had a victory over from the past. Something that bothered me in the past (like something on television) doesn't bother me anymore, or a certain topic of conversation, or thought, or level of intimacy in an inappropriate relationship. Just as cancer can be a silent killer physically, sin can be a silent killer spiritually.

God reminded me—convicted me—that I need to be surrendered to the Spirit daily, letting Him reveal any movement in the wrong direction, any sign of impurity or compromise, any sign of spiritual anemia. I need to love Him enough to want to see it and want to change it. No compromise. God can cure cancer of the body and the soul.

Overwhelmed. During the latter half of the cancer battle, I had many especially challenging days of feeling so sick with post-chemo nausea. At this point, the chemo was making things worse before it could make things better, which was expected.

I had so many needles; I hate needles. I couldn't remember the last time I really slept. On one particular day, it was simply overwhelming. I couldn't take it anymore. I found myself with no option but to just lie there, moaning then crying.

Then God showed up. He used this one particular moment to tell me that He wanted me to use this sense or awareness of being overwhelmed physically to consider being overwhelmed spiritually by Him. This is the depth He wants me to know Him and experience Him. I knew what He meant because I felt it. Then, I felt compelled to listen to my music app. A very timely song just happened to play called—you guessed it—"Overwhelmed" by Big Daddy Weave. God can, and will, use any tool He wants to convey His message. One of the verses in this song is, *"I delight myself in You, In the glory of Your presence, I'm overwhelmed, I'm overwhelmed by You."* Such powerful words! God used this song to overwhelm me with His presence. I no longer thought about nausea; I thought about how amazing God is. My negative physical reality turned into a beautiful spiritual reality.

It is an amazing experience to be overwhelmed by God. It helps to know what being overwhelmed by anything feels like for comparison. I would not appreciate being overwhelmed with God if I did not know what being overwhelmed by something negative felt like. I believe God is always bigger than anything I face. Nothing is too difficult for Him. There is no physical experience that He cannot overcome with His spiritual presence-none. I get to choose what or who I am overwhelmed by. If I don't choose, my enemy will try to choose for me. God wins in overwhelming victory!

Conversational Jesus. I admit that, in the past, when I was awake in the middle of the night when I shouldn't have been,

I would choose to spend this time unproductively by getting up and watching nothing in particular on TV, surfing social media, or playing games on my iPad. Or, I would stay in bed, tossing and turning, and wind up complaining or throwing a pity party. Many times my thoughts or feelings would turn in a negative direction.

One particular night, I was not only awake, but I could barely move from pain and shear fatigue, again. I was awake again when I didn't want to be. I wished I could sleep. Then God showed up. I heard Him say, "Debbie, give me these times when you lay awake. I never sleep or slumber. I am always waiting for you, waiting to speak with you." I hadn't even started praying yet, actually. <u>God</u> started the conversation! Imagine that! God wants to spend time with me, to talk to me! In fact, He is <u>waiting</u> to have a conversation with me. I am learning to "turn my head" toward God throughout the day in realization that He waits for me, to talk with me.

Prayer is more important to Him than it is to me because He wants me to talk with Him far more than I ever want to talk to Him. His love is that much greater. I only love Him because He first loved me.

Just as in human relationships, communication is key to building stronger relationships. This is the truest with Jesus, the most important relationship I have. This season of battle is teaching me that I need to let God define our communication and what prayer sounds like. He waits to speak and to listen. He is a God who communicates.

A purpose of tears. One particular moment, in great physical agony, I found myself simply crying. It was all I could do. I was sick and tired of being sick and tired. Then God showed up. He brought a Scripture to mind from Psalm 84. I had read this before, but now it had such a deeper meaning. God's Word works that way. It comes alive in new ways for God's purposes.

The whole psalm is about loving the presence of God and how blessed we are when we dwell there. This time reading this psalm, one section stood out: verses 5-7. It reads, "Blessed are those whose strength is in you, who have set their heart on pilgrimage. As they pass through the Valley of Baca they make it a place of springs; the autumn rains also cover it with pools. They go from strength to strength, till each appears before God in Zion" (NIV). This passage is a beautiful allegory of how, even during a battle, perhaps because of the battle, I can know God's presence and provision in a whole new way.

The Valley of Baca is considered by some commentators to be figurative for a journey of difficulty or a painful place, even a battle, and Baca can mean weeping or tears. Even godly people cry.

This passage uses the phrase of passing <u>through</u> the valley, not staying there. Those travelling had already found their strength in God and had their hearts set on making it to their destination-to the place where God dwells. Because their hearts were right with God before and during the journey, they experienced the refreshing blessings of God along the way. Their right relationship with God meant God would be free to show up and provide all the refreshment they needed all along their journey. This continued refreshment gave them more and more strength until they reached their journey's end. Instead of the difficulty, or battle, changing them in a negative way, they were able to change the difficulty into something beautiful, letting God do what only He can do, meeting our needs supernaturally. Even a difficult journey—a battle—can be a blessing in the presence of God. God always wins.

CHAPTER **10**

Visual Aids

———∝———

One value of reading scripture or listening to spiritually sound music is that it becomes stored in memory. God uses memory. It was as I was getting my first ever blood transfusion when a certain song came to mind. I found the song on my app and played it as I continued to watch the infusion. The song was "No Longer Slaves" by Bethel Music. I've heard this song many times, but this time it took on a whole new meaning, clearly why God brought it to mind. One verse in that song says, *"Love has called my name, I've been born again, into a family, your blood flows through my veins."* I was overwhelmed in a new way with Jesus's love for me; that He not only shed His blood for me, but then, as His adopted child, His "blood" is in me by spiritual identity. A spiritual thought came to mind; just as I needed blood to live physically, I continually need Jesus to truly live spiritually. The blood transfusion was life-saving for me many times, physically. Abiding in Christ is spiritually lifesaving, eternally.

Another time God showed up was during a test to see if my heart was strong enough for chemo. This test looks at the heart and nearby blood vessels. It was during this scan that

God showed up again. The tech let me see the screen the whole time and told me what I was looking at. I saw lots of different colors and some dark spots. She pointed to a certain place on the screen and said, "Here is your heart." As she said the words, God showed up. He said, "Debbie, I see and know your heart. I want you to give me all your heart. Those darks spots on the screen represent the areas of your life that are not yet fully surrendered to me." I was reminded right then that my heart still needs more sanctifying work. There are still dark spots of sin. So, looking at the screen, I confessed my known sin and asked the Lord to finish His holy work of making my heart holy, more like His.

One time, He showed up during an MRI. It is important to note that I am very claustrophobic, and I would be in the machine for at least two hours! Yikes! As soon as I was all the way in, I did start to panic. Just a couple seconds later though, God showed up. I heard a familiar voice say, "Debbie, I'm here with you. The reason it is dark is because I have you tucked safely under my wing. You are safe here with me." I pictured a mother swan with her chick. I found myself calm and smiling! In an MRI tube! Only God! Then the loud thumping noise started, which you can hear even with ear plugs. As soon as it started, I heard God say, "That loud sound you hear is like my heartbeat. The reason you hear it so easily is because I am holding you close to my heart because I love you so much." Wow! I found myself in a wonderful time of praise, worship, and thanksgiving. I was so overwhelmed with God's love for me! Then I found myself praying for others I knew, that they too would know God's powerful, intimate love. That's how God's love works. It never stops with me (like a bucket); it flows through me (like a funnel). The next thing I knew, the two and a half hours were over! The tech even asked me why I was smiling. I told him God showed up!

God indeed has a sense of humor. Sometime later, after that long MRI, I had to have another shorter one. This time I actually <u>expected</u> to see God show up based on my previous experience. I love how God works like that! I can expect Him. This time, the MRI was performed at a different facility. Instead of giving me ear plugs, they gave me headphones. The tech told me I could pick my genre of music from a very limited selection; I picked "religious." Close enough.

Unfortunately, the headphones did not work very well, so the thumping sound was really too loud. Then God showed up. To understand how God worked this time, think of a cartoon where one of the characters is in love and their heart is literally leaping out of their chest, possibly even getting bigger with each pulse of love and making a loud thumping sound, like a strong heartbeat. God told me the reason I could hear His heart so loudly this time is because He wanted to give me a new measure of His love for me! His heart was beating out of His chest for me. He wanted me to know His heart-pounding love! I wonder if sometimes I am too grown up for my own good. Or maybe I take God too seriously. I think God loves to laugh, to enjoy, to find pleasure with me.

During a different form of test using a large machine, the instant my eyes were closed, I sensed I was in a familiar place—back under the wing! Just like during that long MRI. I recognized this place immediately and felt instantly safe and at peace. This time, though, when God showed up, He had a different message-a message of intimacy.

This time, as I envisioned myself in the safe darkness of being under the wing, God just slightly lifted His wing to see my face. Picture a mother bird with a baby chick under her wing. She knows it is there; now she just wants to see it face to face, to engage lovingly, intimately. God not only draws me under His wing, but also lifts His wing to look into my face. To the extent you can make eye contact with God, this would be it. Such intimacy!

Then I imagined John (the disciple whom Jesus loved) with his head on Jesus' chest in John 13:25. Only someone intimate with another would do this.

Chapter 11

Victory

—∞—

Many years ago, I was told by a good, Christian friend that I was an angry mom and should seriously consider getting counseling. I never saw it, never noticed. It made some sense now that she brought it up. Right around that time, I had heard my daughter, who was about five years old at the time, riding her tricycle, pretending it had a horn. She said, "Honk, honk! Get out of the way, you jerk!" Yep, that was me.

Not long after, a senior pastor whom I was working for at the time told me that I was the most negative person he had ever met. A pastor; yep. It is true that, back then, I was an angry person with a critical spirit. Some of this was upbringing, most was sin nature. Praise the Lord for life change, for transformation!

One of the many blessings of being a Christ-follower is the hope of being made new into the image of Christ. Spiritual change is a process. How fast change happens depends on me and on God. I imagine the journey is different for each of us. Sometimes the change is so subtle I don't notice until something happens. For me, the biggest transformation I didn't even notice. Others did.

During the cancer battle, I was in the hospital for a week nine times over a four-month period. The short version of the story at this point is that I was very sick, not only from the stage four cancer, but also the effects of the chemo, which sometimes led to a complicating medical condition. There were a lot of needles, and I really hate needles. I mention all this for perspective. Let's just say the cancer battle specifically was really, really challenging.

From the very beginning of this battle, many hospital and medical center staff asked about my positive attitude. Some had never seen a positive attitude in a cancer ward. They did not know what to make of it. The most dramatic story of this took place during round four of chemo.

One late afternoon, a lab tech came in to get a blood sample. By her tone and facial expression, she was clearly angry or was having a really bad day. As she barged in the room, all she said was that she was from the lab and needed to draw some blood and did not make eye contact. As she did her thing, I tried to engage with her, but she was clearly not interested in talking. I asked how she was; she responded with an insincere "fine." I asked about her day. "Busy." Still never making eye contact. She did a pain-free job of getting her sample, and I told her so and thanked her. No response. When she turned and started to leave, I wished her a "blessed day." Then, she hesitated and turned toward me, this time looking me in the eye. She said that she had had a long day and saw a lot of people, both hospital staff and patients; I was the first happy person she met all day. She hesitated, looking away. Turning back, she asked me how I could be happy in a cancer ward, being so sick and all. I started with having faith in Jesus Christ. Apparently that wasn't what she wanted to hear. She cut me off mid-sentence, then yelled at me that she wasn't allowed to talk about religion at work with patients and stomped out of the room. I knew I needed to pray for her. Maybe this was why she was the one to come to my room this day.

I did not plan to witness to her. I had no agenda. I believe God is the "king" of divine appointments. If He wants me to meet someone, I will meet that someone, period. It is up to me to be in the right "place" spiritually to use that appointment well. I don't always see these divine appointments coming. It helps to be ready. Sometimes actions or attitude speak better than, or even before, my words.

I believe God set up this divine appointment because He knew she would hear about Jesus and be prayed for. I think some people just want or need to see that faith in Jesus matters, that hope is real. Sometimes this means they need to see joy in the midst of a battle, especially for someone like her who saw sick, negative people all day. Even healthy people can have a bad attitude.

This particular divine appointment reinforced for me that sharing Jesus with people does not have to begin with preaching. Some folks want to see Jesus in us before they want to hear about Jesus from us. Holy Spirit-empowered joy—joy that earthly logic can't explain—is a powerful tool to get someone's attention and, perhaps, start the conversation about its source, it's reality. It is God working in me and through me for His glory. I now know it is possible to be joyful always! God wins!

For a Christ-follower, the victory isn't limited to anything physical or anything my hands can touch. Ultimately, all battles are spiritual on some level. This is where the true victory lies. Every battle can lead to transformation, testimony, and enlarging God's kingdom, bringing more glory to His name.

Epilogue

―――――∝―――――

*M*y goal of writing *When God Showed Up* was simply to share what I have learned about and experienced with God and how He shows up for battle-that it might be an encouragement to any who are going through a battle now or for those who will go through a battle at some point. It is not too late to prepare; it is not too late to decide who wins.

If you are a Christ-follower, I hope *When God Showed Up* encourages you in your relationship with Jesus to look for how He shows up in your life, even if you are not currently facing a battle. God does not need a battle to show up; He wants our faith and our attention. If I am distracted by the noises of the world, my own sin nature, or the enemy of Christ, I won't be able to hear the still, small voice of a God who does not yell.

He wants to reveal Himself in each of our lives daily, unique to our story. The work you see Him do now as He shows up could be preparation for something later, like David the shepherd, who did not then know what God was up to when he had to fight a lion to protect his sheep, and that God would use this experience for his battle with a giant.

If you are not a Christ-follower, I hope *When God Showed Up* encourages you to consider if now is the time to take a step of faith, to choose trust. I know I was not better off without

God; I believe this is true for you too. Do I understand everything about faith and the spiritual life and how God works? No. But I would rather be in a personal relationship with a God who shows up then alone by myself. I would rather be in a relationship with a God that can and will use all I face to transform me from an angry, critical woman struggling with low self-esteem and self-worth, into the woman I am now becoming, one of joy, a woman who is absolutely convinced of the greatness and love of God in Christ Jesus. This is my story of a God who showed up.

CPSIA information can be obtained
at www.ICGtesting.com
Printed in the USA
LVHW020026160222
711186LV00006B/431